# How Do I Use My Revocable Trust...

## and

## Other Estate Documents, Hand Book.

**By: Richard J. Lutzel, Esq.**

www.LutzelBroadway.com

# Table of Contents

www.LutzelBroadway.com

www.LutzelBroadway.com

Additional Information To

www.LutzelBroadway.com

# ABOUT THE AUTHOR.

Richard J. Lutzel has been licensed to practice law since 1991 and is licensed in multiple states including North Carolina, South Carolina, New York and Washington D.C.

Rick was born and raised on the east end of Long Island, about 75 miles from New York City. He attended college at the State University of New York at Buffalo earning a Bachelor of Arts degree in Business and Communication in 1988. He attended law school at the Syracuse University College of Law where he earned a Juris Doctor degree in 1991. He and his wife relocated to North Carolina in 1997 and have made their home outside of Charlotte for themselves and their three sons.

Rick has practiced in the field of Estate Planning and Asset Protection Planning for over thirty years.

www.LutzelBroadway.com

He takes pride in the fact that he has helped thousands of families have the security and comfort knowing their spouse, children and extended family will be well taken care of when the time comes.

## Lutzel Broadway has offices in:

Charlotte, North Carolina,
Indian Trail, North Carolina,
Mooresville, North Carolina,
Myrtle Beach, South Carolina, and
Pawleys Island, South Carolina

Please call us at 704-540-0103,
Please email us at RLutzel@LutzelGandy.com
or

Visit our website at: www.LutzelBroadway.com

# Why Did I Create a Trust?

You were trying to be responsible and do the right thing for your family so you decided it was time to prepare a Last Will and Testament or possibly a Trust.   But, you weren't quite sure how a Trust works or if there are any real benefits over a Will. You went to an attorney and they explained how a Revocable Living Trust would be better for you and make things much easier of your family when the time comes.  The truth is they were correct.  A Trust is far better than a Will and will make things much easier on your family down the road.  So, you commissioned the attorney to draft the legal documents and now you have a Trust. You probably spent a few thousand dollars on their estate planning package, have a great looking set of documents and… now what?  I can't tell you how many times someone has come to me with a beautiful binder full of documents and no clue as to what it all means or how to use it.  Hopefully, the following will help.

# Section One

# ESTATE PLANNING 101

# TERMS AND TERMINOLOGY

## Formal Definitions:

**Attorney In Fact.** If you have a Power of Attorney wherein you designate another individual to act on your behalf, that individual is called an "Attorney In Fact". They are also sometimes called an "Agent In Fact".

**Assignment of Personal Property.** A document that, by general reference terms, adds assets and/or property that does not have a legal title or certification, into your Revocable Living Trust.

**Beneficiary.** A person who derives advantage from something, or is the recipient of an asset from another individual or entity, especially from a Trust, Will, or life insurance policy.

**Certification of Trust.** A certification of trust (or "trust certificate") is a short document signed by the trustee and, in some states, the attorney, that simply states the trust's essential terms and certifies the trust's authority without revealing private details of the trust that aren't relevant to the pending transaction.

**Distribution.**   The sharing, giving, bequeathing or delivering of your property or assets to another person or entity.

**Durable Power of Attorney.**   A legal document that lets someone designate another person, called an agent or attorney-in-fact, to act on their behalf. "Durable" refers to the fact that the agent retains this authority even if the person who created the durable power of attorney becomes incapacitated. This power ends at death.

**Estate.**   All of the money and property owned by a particular person, especially at death.

**Estate Planning.**   A process where an individual designs a strategy and executes a will, trust, and/ or other documents to provide for the distribution of their assets upon incapacity or death. In addition, many thorough estate plans include planning for healthcare needs near the end of life and guardianship for any children.

**Executor.**   A person you appoint who is responsible for carrying out the legal and financial wishes stated in your will, including the payment of debts, sale of assets, and distributions to beneficiaries. This person plays the same role as an administrator if you had died without a valid will.

**Fiduciary.** A person or institution who is legally responsible to act in the best interest of the person for whom they are or it is serving.

**Funding The Trust.** In order for a Revocable Trust to be effective it needs to be funded. That means you must retitle assets into the name of your Trust. n the trusts & estates context, this means the process of transferring assets to a trust.

**Grantor (or Trustmaker or Trustor or Settlor).** A person who creates a trust.

**Guardian.** A person who looks after and is legally responsible for someone who is unable to manage their own affairs, especially an incompetent or disabled person or a child whose parents have died. A person appointed by a parent who attends to the care of their minor children in the event of the parent's death.

**Health Care Power of Attorney/Proxy.** A Health Care Power of Attorney authorizes someone else to make health care decisions for you on your behalf. A Health Care POA can include end of life directives.

**Intestacy, Intestate.** The situation in which a person dies without a valid will. In this case, the distribution of assets will follow the default state laws of the deceased person's final residence.

**Issue.** The term "Issue" refers to natural born children and adopted children. A legal term for all descendants, including children, grandchildren, great-grandchildren, and so on.

**Joint Tenancy with Right of Survivorship, Joint Ownership with Right of Survivorship.**
A type of ownership in which two or more people own the same asset together, and where at death of a co-owner, the surviving co-owner will become the sole owner of the asset, regardless of the distributions made in the deceased co-owner's Will. The jointly owned asset is transferred immediately at death without requiring court action

**Living Will/Health Care Directive.** A written statement detailing a person's own desires regarding their personal medical treatment in certain circumstances in which they are no longer able to express informed consent.

**No-contest Clause.** A clause in a Will or Trust that a beneficiary who challenges the terms of a Will or Trust forfeits any bequests they have in the existing document. Therefore, a no-contest clause is generally used to discourage Will contests. These clauses are not enforced in all instances or states.

**Payable on Death (or Transfer on Death or Totten Trust).** An arrangement between a bank or credit union and a client that designates beneficiaries to receive all the client's assets upon their death. The immediate transfer of assets is triggered by the death of the client. Generally, the payable on death arrangement takes precedent over the distributions specified within a Will.

**Per Capita Distribution.** A method of distributing estate assets so that each surviving heir in the same generation receives the same proportion of the total assets. For example, say a decedent's assets begins equally divided amongst their children. If a child of the decedent passes away prematurely, the assets allocated to that child are re-allocated to a pool. That pool is equally allocated amongst the entire pool of grandchildren who parents predeceased the decedent. In Latin, this roughly translates to "by head."

**Per Stirpes Distribution.** A method of distributing estate assets so that each branch of the family receives the same proportion of the total assets. For example, say a decedent's assets begins equally divided amongst their children. If a child of the decedent passes away prematurely, the assets allocated to that child stays in their "branch" of the family, and gets equally allocated amongst the children of that particular child. In Latin, this roughly translates to "by branch."

**Pour-Over Will.**       A pour-over will is a legal document that ensures an individual's remaining assets will automatically transfer to a previously established trust upon their death.

**Principal or Corpus of the Trust.**       The real property and personal property in a trust to be used for the benefit of trust beneficiaries, either through distribution or income generation In the trust, the grantor specifies how and when the trustee can use the principal.

**Probate.**       The judicial process whereby a Last Will and Testament is presented in a court of law and proven as a valid public document that is the true last testament of the deceased, or whereby the estate is settled according to the laws of intestacy (if no Will) in the state of residence of the deceased at time of death in the absence of a legal will.

**Revocable Living Trust.**       A revocable living trust is a trust document created by an individual that can be changed over time. Revocable living trusts are used to avoid probate and to protect the privacy of the trust owner and beneficiaries of the trust as well as minimize estate taxes.

**Settlor.**      A Settlor is the person or persons that own or create the Revocable Living Trust.

**Spendthrift Provision.**      A clause in a trust preventing creditors from attaching the interest of the beneficiary in the trust before that interest is actually distributed to them. This means that creditors can only lay claim to assets after distribution to beneficiaries. Often it is used to protect the beneficiaries of a trust.

**Successor Trustee.**    A person or institution who becomes the trustee for a trust if the first choice trustee die, resign, or otherwise become unable to act.

**Testamentary Trust.**      A type of trust that is created at death, usually by the terms of a will. Unlike living trusts, testamentary trusts must go through probate before the trust is created, since, for example, the genuineness and validity of the will, and appointment of an executor still need to be established before the creation of the trust. Although a testamentary trust does not avoid probate, it may serve some of the common desired functionalities of a trust, for example, establishing a trust to leave assets to minor children.

**Testator.**  A person who has made a Last Will and Testament or given a legacy.

**Title.**  The legal right to something. In a real estate context, title refers to ownership of the property, meaning that you have rights to use the property.  To re-title means to change the name from an individual to another individual or to a Trust.

**Trustee or Successor Trustee.**  A person or institution who is responsible for managing any property or assets a grantor transfers into and titles in the name of the trust. The trustee has duties to be loyal, be prudent, be impartial, and to inform the beneficiaries of the trust. The trustee can be the grantor and/ or a beneficiary of a trust in addition to the trustee role.

# Terminology and General Use:

First, a brief explanation of why you really should strategically plan your estate, what is a Last Will and Testament, what is the probate process, and how a Trust works and why it is better than a Will.

The first question is, do you really need to strategically plan your estate? If you were to pass away without a Last Will & Testament or a Revocable Living Trust, your assets would be divided and distributed to your nearest living next of kin in accordance with state statute. However, state statute does not consider anything other than a blood-line relation, so your assets could be divided among your parents, children, siblings, aunts, uncles, cousins, etc. In addition, and probably more importantly, state statute will determine who would care for minor children and manage their assets. In many situations, your children will initially be split up and placed in foster care until the court can determine who can act as a guardian. For some people, they are happy with the state government making those decisions. For those who want to make the decision themselves, you need a Will or a Trust.

# What Is a Will?

A Will is your written document that is signed, notarized and witnessed. Your Will directs how you (not the state) want your property to be distributed at the time of your death. You can change it at any time as it is subject to amendment at any time during your lifetime. With a Will you can also name someone to be the guardian of your children. With a Will, upon your death your beneficiaries must go to court and have the court approve the transfer of assets. This is called "probate" and can take as long as 12 months (or more) to complete. It can also be expensive as the court charges significant fees as will the attorney who will probate your estate.

What is Probate?

With or without a Will, your assets have to go through the "probate" process. Probate is defined by Websters as "the action or process of proving before a competent judicial authority (state court) that a document offered for official recognition and registration as the last will and testament of a deceased person is genuine and can be applied." In plain language that means a judge reviews the terms of your Will, reviews the list or "inventory" of your assets, opens the forum up to anyone who may object to the way your Will is written, and ultimately, the judge decides if the terms of your

Will are satisfactory and can be applied to the distribution of your assets. Probate can be a long (6-12 months), costly process wherein the court reviews, scrutinizes and ultimately decides if and when your assets will be distributed and if the provisions of your Will are to be adhered to. Probate is a public process where anybody in the world can come in and see what was in your estate at the time of your passing as well as challenge the provisions of your Will. You can bypass the probate process with a Revocable Living Trust.

## What Is a Living Trust and What Are The Benefits?

A Revocable Living Trust is an intangible legal entity that comes into existence upon the execution of a Trust Agreement. The Trust Agreement "declares" the provisions of the Living Trust as well as procedures and beneficiaries, to be valid. Once the Trust Agreement is signed by you, the Trust exists. Some states also require that the Trust be notarized, some require that it's witnessed, and some require both. It too directs how you want your property to be distributed at the time of your death. However, with a Trust, you do not need to go through the probate process as the provisions of your Trust enable you to go around the court process. Essentially, the Trust re-titles your assets into the name of your Trust entity while you are alive. This means at your death, your assets are still in the name of the Trust and will automatically transfer to your designated beneficiaries according to the terms of the Trust without the need to go to court. With a Trust, you serve as your own Trustee which means you still control (and own) all of your assets. The Trust will provide for or name a successor Trustee upon your death or incapacity. Judicial (court) intervention is not required. Living Trusts are also used to manage property. If a person is disabled by accident or illness, the successor trustee can manage the trust property. As a result, the expense, publicity, and inconvenience of court-supervised distribution of your estate are avoided.

The Trust is created by the person or persons who own the assets to be placed in the Trust. This person is known as the "Settlor". The person in charge of and authorized to act on behalf of the Living Trust is referred to as the Trustee. Trustees also manage the Trust on behalf of the beneficiaries. A Revocable Living Trust is called a self-trusted Trust. Therefore, you are both the Settlor (also known as "Grantor"), are the Trustee of the Trust and during your lifetime, you are the beneficiary of all Trust assets.

With a living trust you also can have significantly more control over who cares for your children. Provisions can be included to transfer guardianship immediately upon your passing so there is no reason to involve foster care.

When the living trust is properly written and funded you can:

- Avoid probate on your assets;
- Save significant time and money by avoiding probate;
- Plan for the possibility of your own incapacity;
- Control what happens to your children and property after you are gone;
- Use it for any size estate; and
- Prevent your financial affairs from becoming a matter of public record.

For most people, a Trust is a better way to insure your goals in estate planning are achieved. You have more control with a Trust and the distribution of your assets is much more efficient.

# Trust vs. Will Considerations

There are many positive reasons to establish a Trust but do not overlook the fact that it will involve more upfront effort and expense. To determine if you should make the extra effort and invest in the expense of a trust, answer these questions:

Do you have children? A trust allows you to establish provisions specifying when a child will be entitled to any assets held in trust. For example, you can stagger the distribution to your children at different ages. The first distribution could be at age 20, then the next at age 25, etc. There is no required age, it is entirely up to you. I have drafted Trusts where distributions aren't fully made until a beneficiary reaches age 65. That may seem extreme but, it what was right for that family.

You can also direct who would care for your children in your absence. You can name more than one person just in case the first person named is unable to provide the care. You can also name a temporary guardian to care for your children if the person you designate as the permanent guardian is from another geographical area and will need time to come for your kids.

You do not need large assets to benefit from a Trust. A common misconception is that a Trust is only for the mega-wealthy. The truth is a Trust simply makes it easier for your family and beneficiaries at the time of your death because all of the asset transfers have been contemplated and directed. Whether your assets total $25K or $25M, a Trust just makes things easier.

Only after your death do the beneficiaries named in the Trust have rights to the Trust property. The grantor (you) can revoke the Trust at any time during your lifetime. Upon death, the Trust becomes irrevocable and therefore, cannot be changed by anyone, including the new Trustee. Let me repeat that because it is very important. While you are alive you can change or "amend" the Trust at any time. When you pass away the Trust, by state law, becomes "Irrevocable" so the person you named as the Successor Trustee can not change or amend the Trust. The provisions you made in your Trust are now cast in stone and no one can change them.

# IT IS NEVER TOO EARLY TO SET UP AN ESTATE PLAN

Although many people know about estate plans and believe they should have one, more than 50 percent of Americans, and almost 70 percent of parents with young children, do not have wills. Dying without a will or any type of estate plan can be a nightmare for those you leave behind.

Intestacy - dying without a valid will - means that your assets pass to your heirs according to state law. If you die without any type of estate plan, its laws will dictate how your property is divided between members of your family. If you would rather not leave it up to the state and want to have a say in how things are distributed after your death, there is no better time than the present to make your wishes known.

There are many reasons to set up an estate plan:

- **Protecting your assets:** An estate plan can protect your assets from unknown (and known) creditors both after your death and during your life. There are many options available for those who fear losing property due to lawsuits or other unforeseen circumstances.

- **Protecting your heirs and significant others:** State law requires that a guardian be appointed to manage the affairs of minor children after the death of their parents. You can designate who you want that person to be. If you are not married and do not have an estate plan, your significant-other may be left with nothing.

- **Avoiding probate:** The probate process can be time consuming and costly for your heirs. Having an estate plan can help them get through that process quickly and with the least amount of legal hassles. It may also be possible to avoid probate altogether.

- **Avoiding a family feud:** By setting up an estate plan, your heirs are less likely to squabble about who gets what after you are gone. You decide who gets the heirlooms and house, and you decide what amount of inheritance each gets, and when.

- **Reducing tax burdens:** Federal and state laws determine whether estate and inheritance taxes must be paid at your death. As there are frequent changes to tax laws, special attention must be given to the tax implications of your estate plan.

If you do not have a will or an estate plan, consult with a lawyer who is experienced with estate planning law. It is never too early to start planning; do not be one of those who start too late.

# ESTABLISHING AN ESTATE PLAN:

# CHOOSING A TESTAMENTARY OR LIVING TRUST

When people think of estate planning, they often think of setting up a Will. However, a Trust is a very useful and flexible tool that is popular with people establishing estate plans. Trusts can replace or supplement your will, as well as help manage property you own during your lifetime. They can also be tailored to fit your needs and the needs of your family.

A Trust is a legal document that manages assets for a person (the grantor) for the benefit of someone else (the beneficiary). Trusts are often used to legally avoid the probate process. The most common example would be parents setting up a trust to manage the income or sale of their property on behalf of their children. If their home is owned by their trust, upon the death of both parents, the home goes directly to their children without having to go through the probate process.

**Types of Trusts**
There are many types of trusts - each with its own requirements, benefits and drawbacks - the terms of which can be quite confusing:

- Revocable and irrevocable trusts
- Special needs and supplemental needs trusts
- Charitable Remainder Trusts
- Life insurance trust
- Testamentary and living trusts

At a basic level, trusts can be divided into two groups: living trusts and testamentary trusts.

**Living trusts** - sometimes called "inter vivos" trusts - are created and take effect during the lifetime of the grantor. The grantor may "fund" his or her trust with the intention of having its provisions continue past his or her death. For example, a woman who is the owner of a large apartment complex may put the building into the name of her trust. The provisions of her trust may dictate that, during her lifetime, she may receive the rental payments to use as she wishes and, upon her death, the trust pays the rental income to her favorite niece.

**Testamentary trusts** are created only upon the grantor's death. It can be created by operation of a person's will or by the provisions of a separate trust. For example, if the parents of young children suddenly die after setting up such a provision in their wills, a testamentary trust would be created after their deaths, managing the financial affairs of the surviving children until they are old enough to handle such matters themselves.

If you are interested in setting up an estate plan and have questions about trusts, consult with an attorney who is knowledgeable with estate planning law. Your lawyer can help you decide which type of trust is best for you and your heirs.

# Revocable Living Trust

A Revocable Trust (or Living Trust) is created for the purpose of holding ownership to an individual's assets during the person's lifetime, and for distributing those assets after death.

The individual who creates the trust (the grantor) names a person who will serve as trustee and will follow the trust's terms after the grantor dies. While alive, the grantor will usually serve as the trustee and control the assets even though they belong to the trust. The grantor has full control and access of all of the assets when they are the trustee. The grantor can also change the trust at any time.

It is called a living trust because it is created during the grantor's lifetime, and takes effect during the grantor's lifetime. By contrast, a will does not take effect until after death.

Perhaps the biggest advantage of a living trust is that it does not have to go through probate, as does a will. This will save significant time, money and privacy for the grantor and their beneficiaries.

The trust enables the grantor to gift assets to whomever they designate in the same manner that a Last Will and Testament does. There is nothing that you can do with a Will that you cannot do with a trust. However, as explained above, with a trust, you avoid probate. In addition, a trust enables you to distribute assets to whomever you designate in a manner that is more tailored to your goals. For example, you can distribute your assets over time to your beneficiaries. A trust allows you to make a distribution to a beneficiary when that person reaches a certain age, then another distribution when they reach a different age, etc. You do not have to gift all of your assets at one time.

The one drawback to a Revocable Living Trust is that it takes a little more time to draft so the up-front preparation cost will typically be a little higher than drafting a Will.

# Important Things To Know About Your Trust:

1.      A Revocable Living Trust like yours does <u>not</u> have its own Employer Identification Number (EIN); it operates under your social security number.

2.      Any asset that you want to include in the TRUST must be transferred or re-titled into the name of the TRUST.  This may require a formal filing of documents with the County or State, or it may just require a phone call to a fund manager.  If the asset is not formally retitled into the name of the Trust, it will NOT be considered to be in the Trust.

3.      You do not need to prepare/file a separate schedule tax form for your TRUST.  Your TRUST will not pay taxes; they are paid by you personally at your normal tax rate.

4.      You can add assets or subtract assets from your TRUST anytime you choose.  You must sign, obtain or convey the asset as a Trustee, not as an individual.

5.      What assets should be transferred into a
        Living Trust?
Typically, most assets that would be probated are

transferred into the Living Trust. This would include real estate (including homes), business interests, money market accounts, stocks, bonds, mutual funds, precious metals, gems, antiques, artwork, royalty contracts, patents, copyrights, valuable collections and other business interests. Life insurance and annuities should list the Living Trust as the remainder beneficiary. IRAs and 401K's should also list the Living Trust as the remainder beneficiary. Although the IRA and 401K have beneficiaries already named, by re-titling these assets into the Trust it insure the proceeds are distributed in accordance with the terms of the trust. If your insurance, IRA or 401K is not titled into the name of the Trust, the value of the asset will be distributed to the beneficiary as soon as they turn 18 years of age.

Motor vehicles, boats, RV's, motorcycles, etc. that have a title should be placed into your Revocable Living Trust.

There is a whole section of this book devoted to assets to be retitled into the Trust and how is the best way to do it. This is called "funding" your Trust.

6.    You can amend the Trust at any time.

7.    The legal name of your new Trust and the name in which your assets should now be

titled is typically found in one of the first paragraphs on the first page of the Trust Agreement. It will look something like: "The Smith Revocable Trust Dated January 2, 2023".

# Section Two

# HOW TO USE YOUR
# NEW TRUST

# Frequently Asked Questions:

**Do I still need a Last Will and Testament?**    A Revocable Living Trust essentially takes the place of a Last Will and Testament.  When an attorney drafts a Revocable Trust they should also always draft a "Pour-Over Will".  This document basically captures any asset that is not titled into the name of the Trust and instructs the court to distribute the asset under the terms of the Trust.  However, the asset does need to go through probate.

**Can I leave my assets to whomever I want or does the Trust restrict the distributions?**
        Your Trust gives you greater control and flexibility over having a Will or relying on state statute.  That said, the provisions of a Trust that trigger a distribution or a right to ownership, or any other event, does not necessarily be tied to your death.  The vast majority of Trusts are triggered by death but, they don't have to be.  Triggering events can be any life-event that you want.  For example, I can state in my Trust that my son shall receive the title to real estate when he graduates from college.  This type of provision does requiring additional planning and drafting to insure the desired result is achieved.

**Do my beneficiaries receive my assets when the turn 18 years old?** With a Trust, you can stagger distributions over time as your beneficiaries reach certain ages or according to life events or both. You can also withhold distributions if the situation so warrants. For example, if a prospective beneficiary has a substance abuse problem and you do not want to distribute any assets until that person is no longer abusing the substance, you can instruct your Trustee to withhold distributions until they pass three (or any number you choose) drug tests.

**Is the Trust assigned a new tax identification number?** No, the Trust does not have its own tax identification number. This type of Trust and all of the assets retitled into the Trust are still under your social security number(s). There are some Trusts called "Irrevocable Trusts" the are assigned a new tax identification number. A Revocable Living Trust does not get a tax id number.

**Do I have to file additional tax returns?** You do not have to file any additional or any unique tax returns. You file the same way you always have.

**Do I have to file a copy of the Trust with the State, County or City/Town?** No, you do not have to file the Trust with any governmental body. It will have to be given to any financial institution or entity that is holding or managing your assets that you want to retitle. The entity will need to see the Trust or the Certification of Trust, to verify you have the authority to retitle the assets and to name the Successor Trustee if something were to happen to you. I recommend that you keep the original Trust in a safe place but NOT a Safety Deposit Box at the bank. The reason is if something happens to you and you are the only key holder or authorized user of the box, you will need a court order to open it. I suggest buying a small, fire-proof safe to be kept in your home.

**Should I give a copy of the Trust to my Successor Trustee?** Whether or not you want to give a copy of the Trust to someone else is up to you. I can tell you that if you give someone a copy, they are likely to read it and, at this point, it may be none of their business. I recommend telling your Successor Trustee where the Trust is located and how to access it but, I do not recommend giving them a copy. However, I recommend giving your Successor Trustee a copy of the Certification of Trust.

**How does the guardian gain custody of my children if something happens to me?** The guardian should also know where the original Trust is located and how to access it. I also recommend giving the Guardian of your children a copy of the Certification of Trust. This legally binding document grants custody to the Guardian named in your Trust.

**How does my Trust become funded?** A Trust that is not funded is worthless. To "fund" your Trust you must re-title your assets into the name of the Trust. In the pages to follow we explain how to fund your Trust.

# How to Fund Your Living Trust:

Signing a Living Trust isn't the end of estate planning; you also need to fund the Trust. A Revocable Living Trust that is not funded is worthless. Knowing how to fund a Living Trust is vital for the Trust to accomplish its goals.

Funding a Living Trust involves transferring property to the Trust. An asset not transferred to the Trust is not owned by the Trust and will be subject to probate (unless you've used another technique to avoid probate). In short, if there are no assets in the Living Trust, there is no Living Trust. How to fund a Trust varies depending upon the nature of the property. You can transfer ownership, or, in some cases, designate the Trust as a beneficiary upon your death.

To fund a trust with your bank accounts, you will retitle the accounts into your trust's name. You should sign new signature and ownership cards to retitle any accounts or cash equivalents, including treasury bills, money market accounts, and certificates of deposit, into your Trust. You do NOT need to open a new account or a Trust Account. You are retitling your existing account from your personal name to the Trust's name, with you as Trustee.

Before you retitle your certificates of deposit, consult with a bank officer to make sure that the institution does not consider the change in account name to be an early withdrawal that incurs a penalty. Generally, this should not be a problem because your tax identification number for the account will remain the same.

Instruct your financial institution by letter (samples are attached at the end of this section) or in person to change the title to your Trust. The tax identification number (your Social Security number) on the account will remain the same. There is no new Tax ID, EIN, or TIN for the Trust. For joint trustee trusts, be sure to give each trustee signature power with respect to the account. Sign the new signature cards as "Trustees".

When you retitle an account, it should have no effect on the name you wish to have printed on your checks. There is no reason to have the name of your trust on your printed checks. Ask your bank to continue to print your individual name on the checks. As an outsider looking at your accounts, that person should not be aware that your account is held by a trust at all, but should appear that everything is still titled in your name.

Many credit unions will not allow clients to retitle their account due to charter provisions. Originally, credit unions were created to cater to a specific group of people (i.e- Delta Community was originally only Delta Airlines employees). These days credit union charters have often been expanded to allow members of the general public to bank with them, but their charters may not have expanded to include Revocable Trusts. If your credit union does not allow you to retitle your account into your Trust, simply name the Trust as Payable on Death (P.O.D) beneficiary, which still avoids probate and assures the account passes to the Trust upon your death.

www.LutzelBroadway.com

# The Title Of The Trust

Your Trust document has a title of: "(Your Name) as Trustee and (Your Spouse's Name) as Trustee of The Name of The Trust." The official name of your Trust will be used on deeds, certificates of title, and assignment of interest documents, as well as on beneficiary designations. The legal name of the Trust is typically found in one of the first paragraphs on the first page of the Trust Agreement.

.

### 1. Transfer Real Estate

Transferring real property to a Trust requires a new deed be filed with the County Register of Deeds office. Your attorney's office can file a Quit Claim Deed on your behalf. The deed needs to be signed, with the required witnesses, and also be notarized. You may need to file a copy of the Trust document, or the Certification of Trust. It is preferable to file the Certification of Trust (if you have to file anything) because it is only two or three pages and avoids having the details of the Trust document in the public record.

## 2. Transfer Titled Personal Property

If personal property has a title document (ie. cars, trucks, motorcycles, RVs, ATVs, boats, airplanes), it is encouraged to transfer the title to show the Living Trust as the owner. This will require a trip to the DMV and file a new title. The existing title is signed and notarized as if you are selling the vehicle, but the transferee will be your Trust.

> **\*Caution**: Consult your insurance agent if a transfer will affect your premiums.

## 3. Fund Untitled Personal Property

Personal property without a title document (furniture, books, jewelry, tools, collectibles, etc.), is transferred with an assignment of ownership through a provision in the Trust. This is typically a stand-alone document that your attorney will have drafted with your Trust Agreement.

## 4. Transfer Bank Accounts

Your bank can tell you how savings, checking, and money market accounts can be titled in your Trust.

It should be as simple as changing the title of ownership to your Trust.

If you want to do this with a Certificate of Deposit (CD), be sure that your bank won't consider this an early withdrawal and assess penalties. You can wait for the CD to mature, then open a new CD for the Trust, or change the beneficiary to the Trust.

### 5. Fund Securities

Your broker or fund manager can advise you how to retitle a brokerage account, mutual fund or have stock and bond certificates reissued into the name of your Trust.  A nonqualified annuity can also be retitled, or the Trust can be made a beneficiary. Remember, do not change the title on 401Ks or IRAs.  You are advised to change the second beneficiary on your 401K or IRA so you do not trigger a penalty or a tax.  *See Item 10 below for IRA's, 401K's, etc.*

### 6. Transfer Business Interests

Interests in partnerships and LLCs, and shares in a corporation, can be retitled in the name of the Trust.

Check the partnership agreement, LLC operating agreement, or articles of incorporation, for transfer restrictions or procedures. A document called an "Assignment" is often times used to transfer interest in an LLC. Our office can prepare the Assignment if it is needed.

## 7. Change Life Insurance Beneficiaries

Your Trust can be the owner and/or the beneficiary of a life insurance policy. Making the Trust the owner allows the **Trustee** to manage the policy in the event you become mentally incapacitated, such as borrowing against the policy to obtain funds for your care. Alternatively, list the Trust as the beneficiary as this will insure the insurance proceeds are distributed according to the terms (and ages) of your Trust.

## 8. Transfer Royalties, Copyrights, Patents, and Trademarks

Whoever pays the royalties can advise you what is required to transfer the interest to your Trust. Consult the United States Copyright Office for copyrights, and the United States Patent and Trademark Office for patents and trademarks.

## 9. Accounts Receivable

An assignment of rights - a legal document changing who has the right to a debt - can make your Trust the recipient of payments received on loans you have made to anyone (such as an unsecured personal loan or a loan secured by a mortgage).

## 10. Tax Deferred Accounts (IRA, 401K, 403K, etc.)

One option is to list your spouse as the primary beneficiary, and then list your TRUST as the contingent or (secondary beneficiary). Why would someone choose to do that?

Arranging it that way would allow your spouse to essentially assume/inherit your 401k balance in the form of a tax-free rollover into an IRA that is treated as their very own IRA. At your death, your 401k money would be rolled directly over into your spouse's IRA, and they would then would have distribution options that are quite a bit more flexible than if the TRUST was listed the primary beneficiary.

A surviving spouse is treated in a special way. Surviving spouses get to treat tax-qualified inherited spousal assets (from a 401k, 403b, or IRA) as their own, so they can choose to continue to hold the money in their own IRA for a much longer timeframe. Their distribution options are tied to their own specific life-expectancy. Their specific age dictates how fast & how much they would have to eventually be taken out as a Required Minimum Distribution. Surviving spouses can delay taking any money out of their IRA until they turn 72, (or even longer if they are still working after that age). This allows them to defer paying taxes on the assets for decades & decades (assuming they are a long way away from turning age 72).

When a beneficiary of your retirement plan is ANYONE OTHER than your spouse, (like a TRUST, or your kids, or your siblings, grandkids, etc.) then the inherited money effectively goes into an "Inherited IRA" & doesn't have nearly the same degree of flexibility that a spousal IRA does. Non-spousal inherited IRAs are subject to a 10 year distribution requirement (which means the money has to fully come out of the IRA as taxable income within 10 years). Because of this, it can't grow/compound in a tax deferred way for very long at all.

For this reason, many times I recommend keeping a spouse as the primary and list the Trust as the secondary beneficiary.

Either way you go, whether the Trust is named as the Primary or the secondary beneficiary, you would enter your own SSN when asked/prompted for the Tax ID of the Trust.

By transferring your assets into your Living Trust, you bring them under the legal protection of this estate planning tool. Once the Trust is funded, the assets it holds will be protected from probate.

# Section Three

# ESTATE ADMINSTRATION MANUAL

www.LutzelBroadway.com

# WHAT TO DO WHEN SOMEONE PASSES AWAY.

Losing a loved one can be incredibly difficult, both emotionally and logistically.

The experience often comes suddenly and is certain to cause a flood of overwhelming emotions.

While everyone processes grief differently, it's fairly typical for most people to get confused or be uncertain around what "next steps" may be required legally.

Whether these tasks apply to you as a close friend or family, or you're assisting the named executor who is formally in charge of managing the estate—

Here is the ultimate checklist for all of the important things that need to be considered after losing a loved one.

# What To Do Immediately After Someone Dies

## 1. Check in with immediate family and get support

This can be a difficult first phone call or message, both to make or to receive. Every family is different and there is no right process for who should be called first except that sharing the news "sooner, rather than later" is generally the best practice.

Emotions and others responses to the news may vary widely. Offer your support when able, but be sure to protect your own emotions and natural response as well.

## 2. Make immediate plans.

Depending on whether your loved one passed away in their own home, hospice, or in a hospital, different plans may need to be made in order to arrange proper care of the body.

Check any driver's license, living will, or advance directive to verify whether she or he was an organ donor. If so, quickly call the nearest hospital as certain organs must be collected within a limited time-period in order to ensure a successful donation.

Arrange for the immediate care of any people or pets that your loved one was responsible for until further long-term arrangements can be made.

## 3. Notify close family, friends and work

It's typical to notify family first, starting with those family members who had the closest relationship. Afterwards, contact any known friends, co-workers or employers.

Welcome any offers from others to help share the news with others who will want to know.

## 4. Honor end of life wishes (if known)

Many individuals express their wishes for end of life arrangements ahead of time with a last will & testament, advance directive, or other medical document.

Other times, these wishes may have been communicated verbally to one's significant other, children, or even healthcare staff such as their doctor, nurse or a death doula.

If no wishes have been documented or otherwise communicated, discuss options with the closest family members in order to make a decision on what arrangements seem most appropriate.

Be sure to take into account any religious preferences or cultural norms.

## 5. Select appropriate funeral, burial, or cremation provider to plan ceremony

Identify and work with a funeral home, crematory or cemetery to plan for and facilitate any end of life celebrations or funeral ceremonies.

Like most things these days, there are incredible resources online which can be an excellent starting place for guidance, support and inspiration. For those who prefer a personalized approach, it can be really helpful to work with an independent funeral consultant.

Either way, these resources can be tremendously helpful in understanding available options, saving time & money, and allowing the family to focus

www.LutzelBroadway.com

more energy towards honoring one's life and taking care of one another.

These days, its also widely accepted to use online technology to better allow for digital participation or attendance of end of life celebrations for family or friends who live far away or otherwise have medical or age-related challenges with attending in-person.

## 6. Decide on a couple charities that honor your loved one's legacy

It's very common these days for friends and family to express their condolences by purchasing flowers, making donations to a designated charity or sending other sympathy gifts in lieu of flowers.

These decisions are generally included within the obituary, mentioned during any funeral ceremonies or shared online if using an online memorial service like LifeWeb360.

## 7. Publish obituary and notice to creditors

Draft an obituary with the help of family and friends or by using an online obituary writing tool. Keep in mind you'll typically pay "for each line of text" of any obituary posted in local newspapers, so it's a good idea to make those as short as possible.

Longer obituaries can always be published online for free or distributed directly to friends and family if being used as keepsake honoring one's life accomplishments and legacy.

## 8. Locate or identify their Trust or their Last Will & Testament

Individuals often update their last will & testament based upon impactful financial or family-based life changes, so be sure to review the dates and titling of any legal documents you find in order to ensure what you've found contains one's most recent wishes.

Interpreting these documents can often be challenging, especially following an emotionally traumatic loss, so consult an attorney or self-help platform as needed.

If the documents appear to be drafted, or signed by a law firm, it's a good idea to call their office to alert them of the passing and ask for any other documents your loved one may have on file.

**Tip:** if your loved one has ever lived or owned property in other states, you may discover multiple documents, from multiple attorneys, covering local laws from multiple states. This can feel very intimidating, but find comfort in knowing that each document is originally written for a particular reason and once everything is found and organized, these documents will make a lot more sense.

## 9. Notify anyone named the Will and set initial expectations

Now is not the time to stress over interpreting one's will, though it can be helpful to at least initiate a conversation with anyone named in the document to let them know.

Setting the right expectations is very important since this will likely be a first-time experience for you or any heirs/beneficiaries.

For now, simply let them know who will be working with them (typically named "executor" or "personal representative" within documents) and ask for their patience as getting started with navigating the responsibilities to follow is typically a slower process than expected or portrayed in pop-culture.

In these early conversations, it's entirely okay to not have, or be able to provide, exact answers if pressed by family members.

If no will can be found, intestacy laws will apply and next steps can be outlined by the local probate judge, or probate clerk, within the County of your loved one's primary residence.

## 10. Pause and take some time to grieve, mourn and self-care

Grief has many stages (5 to be exact) and it's easy to get distracted by "all of the things to get done." So much that the sudden waves of changing emotions can quickly become overwhelming.

Make sure you have a support group or healthy outlet for mourning and properly processing your feelings.

Online resource centers such as Love Lives On not only provide incredibly helpful content, but can also help connect you with professional resources available in your area.

Self-care is a vital step… both initially and over the weeks, months and years to follow.

# Next Steps After A Funeral

## 11. Secure valuables, personal assets, & belongings

It's unfortunate, but knowledge that someone has passed away can be an invitation for theft, either from criminals, or even well-intentioned family members wanting to claim sentimental or financially valuable items.

It's good practice to change locks on the home and ensure all windows or doors can be properly closed or secured.

Walk through the home to remove any perishable items from the kitchen, wash any clothes or bed linens, and clean any bathrooms if the home will be unoccupied for a while.

Don't forget to check under mattresses or within coat pockets in the closet to find any cash that might be hidden and find a safe place to store any valuable's like jewelry, car keys or family heirlooms.

Depending on family relationships, it can be worthwhile to ask a trusted friend or family member to join you, not only as an extra set of helping hands, but also as a witness to your actions to help prevent any family disputes or accusations.

## 12. Helping hands from friendly neighbors

Ask a neighbor or nearby friend to keep a watch over the home for any evidence of unusual activity or to help avoid any obvious signs that the home is unoccupied, such as the overflow of mail, amazon deliveries or newspapers piling up near the front door.

## 13. Identify and involve any named executors or personal representatives

Get in touch with any individuals named within the will to be in charge of settling or administering the estate.

This is commonly a surviving spouse, child, or trusted friend and could also involve multiple people serving together as co-executors.

While being named as the executor or personal representative over one's estate is a big honor and testament of a trusted relationship, it can also require a considerable amount of time and work.

Being named does not create a requirement for that person to accept or serve, so conversations should be had with any named individuals to discuss the responsibilities involved and gauge one's willingness (or ability) to act.

## 14. Leverage estate settlement resources to help simplify the process

Being a personal representative or executor can become quite expensive depending upon the details of the estate, family relationships & local laws. Particularly since it's a relatively unfamiliar process that individuals only go through once or twice during their lives (hopefully).

In fact, families often spend a minimum average of $14,000 when hiring professional advisors.

Better yet, many choose to make use of DIY platforms which offer individualized step-by-step guidance, helpful tools, access to necessary forms and the ability to automatically generate shareable reports designed to decrease the amount of time, money and stress spent working through the process.

## 15. Determine if probate is necessary

The probate process isn't one-size-fits-all, but rather, may occur in different ways depending upon the location, type or probate required, ownership & titling of assets and the overall fair market value of assets left behind in the estate.

While there are more in-depth guides available which outline and de-mystify probate, it's important to get an initial assessment of whether probate will be necessary, and if so, whether the estate may qualify for an accelerated probate before obtaining "letters" in order to avoid costly or timely mistakes later in the process.

Be sure to check the way certain assets are titled in order to assess whether they will fall into probate or should pass directly to known beneficiaries.

## 16. Obtain letters & present will to the probate court (if there is one)

In order to authorize transactions or direct action by institutions, agents or advisors holding access to assets of the estate, you'll need to either obtain "letters testamentary" or "letters of administration" by visiting that old courthouse building downtown.

While visiting the probate court can be an unfamiliar (or downright anxious) experience for some, keep in mind that the actual probate clerks and judges who work there are sensitive to your situation and trained to help.

That said, because the clerk staff are not attorneys, keep in mind that they're unable to provide any individualized guidance which could be misunderstood as legal advice.

# Things To Do Within the First 30 Days

If you hire an attorney, they will take care of some of the next steps.

## 17. Notify the IRS and obtain a Tax ID number for the estate

Once someone has passed away their individual social security number loses its effective purpose and value. As a result, a new tax ID number must be obtained from the IRS in order to *authorize* activities on behalf of the estate.

This new number is commonly referred to as an E.I.N., which technically means "employer identification number," though it can be more helpful to think of it as the "estate identification number."

Either way, this new estate E.I.N. can be applied for online, by FAX or mail, and will ultimately be used to close the estate when filing the final Form 1041 tax form.

## 18. Publish a notice to creditors

The public posting of a notice to creditors is the formal process for informing any creditors of the estate of their opportunity to submit any unpaid bills or outstanding debt of the estate.

Local laws determine the format and frequency of publishing these notices in order to ensure effectiveness. As such, it's helpful to use online tools to help automate the process.

If this process is overlooked or skipped, it's possible for creditors to surface months or even years afterwards with a legal right to demand payment t hereby forcing heirs to reopen the estate.

## 19. File a request to forward mail

Filing a request with the local post office to arrange for forwarding of mail addressed to the deceased is generally pretty simple, although it will require proper documentation showing your legal capacity to act over the estate.

This process can be tremendously helpful for surfacing any unpaid bills, active subscriptions or accounts that should be closed.

Although it's not required, many publishers of magazines or subscriptions will even issue a refund for any unused subscription services– so be sure to inform them of the situation.

## 20. Register for DMA "Do Not Contact" List

The Data & Marketing Association (DMA) maintains a Deceased Do Not Contact List (DDNC) for the sole purpose of requiring all DMA members to remove the names and addresses of deceased individuals from all marketing lists.

There is no fee or cost to register online for the Deceased Do Not Contact List, and only takes about 2 minutes, so this is a really good way for family members, friends or executors to reduce the amount of marketing & advertising materials (a.k.a. "junk mail") being received by mail. The DDNC records are updated and distributed to members monthly, so don't be surprised if it takes 2 or 3 months to begin noticing the effect of receiving less mail.

Either way, taking a moment to register for the Do Not Contact List is an important step in minimizing the risk of future identify theft or fraud abuse.

For any materials which continue to arrive, you can notify these companies by simply writing "Deceased, Return to Sender" and leaving the envelope in the mailbox for the postmaster to return.

## 21. Notify insurance and financial institutions

If your loved one had a life insurance policy, it's important to alert the carrier of the death and begin the process of submitting a claim against the policy.

With banks and financial institutions, we recommend calling each institution ahead of time to pre-arrange a conversation, or meeting, with a manager-level employee to save time by making sure they're familiar with the internal procedures for handling these conversations.

During these pre-planning calls, be sure to ask what specific documentation they will require before discussing details of the account with you, and whether these documents (like death certificates) must be originals or can be certified copies.

## 22. Open new bank account, and transfer or retitle assets

Depending upon the type of account and whether it was co-titled or shared with another individual, remaining funds must generally be transferred into a new account titled in the name of the estate.

This new bank account will also serve as the checking account used to pay any ongoing bills such as mortgages, utilities, or receive funds like unearned wages.

Be sure to access any safe deposit boxes in order to inventory the contents, or open a new security box to safe-keep any valuables found within the home.

## 23. Cancel services, utilities, driver's licenses, SSN, & voter's registration

If not already done by the funeral home, someone will need to contact the social security office to report the death and apply for any survivor's benefits. These reports cannot be made online, so instead, you will need to call the applicable social security local field office or the national help number: 1-800-772-1213.

To further help prevent fraud or identity theft, you should also cancel any driver's licenses, voter's registrations & unused services or accounts such as cable, internet & monthly subscriptions.

*...Wait, risk of identity theft after death?*

Yep, you heard that right. In fact you might be surprised, but fraudsters' often use techniques like "ghosting" to strike victims after death, causing a nightmare of problems for surviving family members.

# 24. Identify and pay important bills or outstanding claims

Keep track of any bills or claims paid by the estate or payments received, such as unearned income or social security benefits.

This accounting will be important for sharing as an accurate and transparent reporting to the probate court, advisors, family and on income tax forms of the estate.

It can be helpful to also indicate which bills are ongoing (such as utilities, rent/mortgage, credit cards or car loans).

Not only will this help ensure the bills are paid on time, but also provides a great way to monitor usage and assess when these services can be cancelled if being unused (i.e. cable, phone & internet services).

## 25. Compile inventory of all assets

One of the largest responsibilities of an executor is compiling a complete inventory of all assets in the estate and their estimated fair market value.

While this is formally required for determining whether probate is necessary or what inheritance taxes may be due, it's also a best practice to help minimize the likelihood of arguments among family members.

For many items, especially those with sentimental value or similar descriptions such as jewelry, collectibles or family heirlooms, it can be really helpful to include pictures of the asset within the inventory report to help avoid confusion.

Estate settlement platforms like Atticus help make this as simple as snapping a photo of assets to be uploaded into the report automatically.

www.LutzelBroadway.com

## 26. Tackle the digital footprint

Many online or digital platforms have a unique process outlined for closing an account, while others like Facebook simply allow others to memorialize the account.

Be sure to talk with family members to reach an agreement before any accounts are closed, especially if you're able to download or save any data. This is also true for email accounts.

Also, don't forget to look for any files, purchased media or pictures stored on computer hard drives or cloud storage accounts.

# Things To Do Within The First Six Months

## 27. Make a decision about compensation for the executor

Though not required, many individuals (and effectively all attorneys or professional executors) elect to take some compensation based upon the amount of work involved.

Each state has its own laws around the maximum fees allowable, which is generally based upon a combination of the value of the assets, degree of complexity and overall time involved.

It's helpful to review these laws, or use an online executor fee calculator, to help determine what compensation is allowable for your situation before deciding whether or not to claim the fee.

## 28. File returns & pay any taxes

Generally, a Form 1040 individual income taxes will need to be filed for the portion of year covering Jan 1st until the date of passing. Additionally, an IRS Form 1041 "estate" income tax return will need to be filed covering the remaining portion of the year from the date of death until Dec 31st, and annually thereafter until the estate is closed.

Depending on the primary residence of the individual, state income tax returns may also be required– again, both for the individual and for the estate.

It's important to be aware that other death taxes exist and should be considered, such as estate tax or inheritance tax. In reality, these are uncommon as the exemption amounts are set very high and therefore generally only apply to a small minority of very large estates, particularly at the federal level.

Although many people use the terms "estate tax" and "inheritance tax" interchangeably, they are not the same thing and have a few differences.

Generally speaking, an estate tax is a state or federal tax on the overall value of an estate and is payable by the estate, whereas an inheritance tax is based only on the value of inheritance received by a beneficiary from the estate, with the beneficiary being responsible for paying the applicable tax not the estate.

There is no federal inheritance tax and only a handful of states impose one (Iowa, Kentucky, Maryland, Nebraska, New Jersey & Pennsylvania).

## 29. Distribute assets to heirs & beneficiaries

Once you feel confident that all claims have been settled and taxes paid, the personal representative can begin to distribute any remaining assets to named heirs & rightful beneficiaries of the estate.

## 30. Final report & close the estate

Upon final distribution of the estate's assets, and assuming no ongoing family disputes or creditor claims exists, a final estate inventory reporting can be filed with the probate court in order to officially complete the process and close the estate.

As is customary with most legal or tax-sensitive documents, it's recommended (or pseudo required) to keep all statements, accountings, forms and tax returns for a period of 7-10 years.

# Section Four

# HOW TO USE A POWER OF ATTORNEY

www.LutzelBroadway.com

# How Do I Use a Power of Attorney?

A power of attorney (POA) is a legal document that is signed, witnessed and notarized. This document allows someone (as an attorney-in-fact/agent) to act for and on behalf of another person (the principal). Once the document is signed and properly notarized and/or witnessed, it conveys a legal authority to another individual to act on your behalf. The power can vary from narrow to broad, temporary to permanent, effective immediately, or for the future.

One of the biggest advantages of having a Power Of Attorney is the convenience factor. Your attorney can act on your behalf to handle your affairs without you being present. If you are unable to carry on your own business due to a physical disability, a mental disability or if you are simply in another geographical location, you Agent in Fact can make sure your business is handled.

Having a Power of Attorney in place can be a comfort knowing your affairs can be kept in order even if you are unable to do it yourself.

There are some disadvantages which is why you must be very careful in whom you designate to be your Attorney In Fact.  The Attorney In Fact has the authority to bind you legally as if you had signed a document yourself.  Anything the Attorney In Fact does on your behalf is as legally binding as if you were sitting there and signing the document personally.

Make no mistake, a Power of Attorney and the authority it conveys can, and has been abused.  Again, it is important to give careful consideration to who you convey the authority.

With the above-mentioned potential for abuse or fraud in mind, many third parties, such as a bank or other financial institution, may not accept a power of attorney.

Things to Consider When Drafting a Power of Attorney:

If your POA is going to have great control over finances, the agent-principal relationship should be comprised of the utmost trust.

www.LutzelBroadway.com

A child under the age of 18 years cannot act as you fiduciary or Attorney (or Agent) In Fact.  The designee must be of the age of majority.

Your Attorney In Fact must be able to prove their identification with a valid, unexpired, photo identification.

The original Power of Attorney document must be filed or "recorded" in the county in which you are domiciled (reside).  You can use the recorded POA in any jurisdiction as long as it is on record in your County of Residence.  You should give a date-stamped photocopy of the Power of Attorney to any entity or institution in which you intend to use the POA.  I recommend providing a copy to your local bank(s), financial planner, attorney and anyone else whom your Attorney in Fact may need to be in contact with on your behalf.

Banks and other institutions may have their own manner in which your Attorney In Fact must sign your name when acting on your behalf.  Often times it includes a significant amount of verbiage beyond simply signing your name.  I would check with the institution before signing any document to be sure it is done as they so desire.

A Power of Attorney can have a termination date included in the document itself.  If there is a date of termination stated, the document will automatically, by law, become null and void upon the date being reached.  If there is no date of termination date state in the document, the only way to terminate the Power of Attorney is in writing and then recording the Termination document with the county where the original Power of Attorney was filed.  I strongly recommend providing a copy of the termination document to every institution to whom the original POA was first given.

A Power of Attorney, by law, becomes null and void upon your passing.

# Section Five

# FORMS AND WORK SHEETS

# EXAMPLE FUNDING LETTER

January 1, 2023

TRUST FUNDING LETTER TO:

Fidelity Investments
123 Company Street
Charlotte, North Carolina 28277

RE: Account Number(s): 000987612345

Dear Sir or Madam:

Please transfer the title to the above account(s) into our Revocable Living Trust. Title should be held exactly as follows:

**John Smith, Trustee and Jane Smith, Trustee of The Smith Revocable Trust.**

Since the Trustee(s) of this Trust are also the Grantor(s), no new tax identification number is required and the account name should be reported under the social security number of either trustee, which should be on file. [IRC Reg. Sections 1.671-4(b), 1.6012-3(a)(9), 301-6109-1(a)(2)1.]

EFFECT ON ACCOUNT: These transfers should not affect interest, dividends, life insurance or any other income

www.LutzelBroadway.com

on the investments. If transfers will in any way affect income, dividends or life insurance please contact us prior to making changes. These transfers should also not affect the language on our checks, if a checking account is involved.

ONE SIGNATURE REQUIRED: PLEASE NOTE THAT the trust authorizes either trustee to sign alone on any account.

CAUTION REGARDING TAX-DEFERRED ACCOUNTS: Do not transfer ownership of IRA, 401K, 403K or other tax-deferred accounts into the trust.

The account address should remain the same as currently on file.

Thank you for your assistance in this matter.


John Smith, Trustee       Jane Smith, Trustee

# Legacy Plan and Inventory of Assets

The next section is the Legacy Plan and Inventory of assets. This section gives you the opportunity to list the people or entities in your life that you would want notified if something were to happen to you. This can include family, friends, co-workers, medical personnel, government authorities, etc.

This section also gives you the opportunity to list or inventory your assets. You can indicate what the asset is, where it is, who the contact person is if there is one, an account number, password, PIN, etc. Basically, the information your Successor Trustee will need to access your assets if they needed to. Remember, if your assets aren't identified or discovered by your Successor Trustee or beneficiaries, those assets will "escheat" or be given to the state. It is important to make sure your loved ones know where and how to locate and claim your assets.

# INVENTORY OF ASSETS AND LEGACY PLAN OF

_____

**AND**

_____

This Inventory of Assets and Legacy Plan includes additional steps to take upon the passing of a loved one. It includes all or at least most of the information that will be needed to put their estate plan into motion. The information contained herein is very sensitive and should be kept very secure.

The estate documents that will be needed are contained in this book. The pertinent information that will also be needed is contained herein as well.

Name: _____

Date of Birth: _____

SS# _____


Name: _____

Date of Birth: _____

SS#: _____

# CONTACT INFORMATION OF PEOPLE TO BE NOTIFIED

## HEALTH CARE PROVIDERS, HOSPICE, ETC. TO NOTIFY

Name: _____

Email:_____

Phone: _____


Name: _____

Email:_____

Phone: _____


Name:_____

Email:_____

Phone: _____

www.LutzelBroadway.com

Name: _____

Email:_____

Phone: _____


Name: _____

Email:_____

Phone: _____


Name:_____

Email:_____

Phone: _____


Name:_____

Email:_____

Phone: _____

## FRIENDS AND FAMILY TO NOTIFY

Name: _____

Email:_____

Phone: _____


Name:_____

Email:_____

Phone: _____


Name: _____

Email:_____

Phone: _____


Name: _____

Email:_____

Phone: _____

Name: _____

Email:_____

Phone: _____


Name: _____

Email:_____

Phone: _____


Name: _____

Email:_____

Phone: _____


Name: _____

Email:_____

Phone: _____

# INVENTORY OF ASSETS

## Life Insurance Policies:

Name of Insurance Carrier: _____

Name of Insurance Agent: _____

Contact Info: _____
Policy Number: _____

Location of policy: _____


Name of Insurance Carrier: _____

Name of Insurance Agent: _____

Contact Info: _____
Policy Number: _____

Location of policy: _____

Name of Insurance Carrier: _____

Name of Insurance Agent: _____

Contact Info: _____
Policy Number: _____

Location of policy: _____


Name of Insurance Carrier: _____

Name of Insurance Agent: _____

Contact Info: _____
Policy Number: _____

Location of policy: _____


Name of Insurance Carrier: _____

Name of Insurance Agent: _____

Contact Info: _____
Policy Number: _____

Location of policy: _____

# Bank Accounts:

## Savings and Checking Accounts:

Name of Bank: _____

Type of Account: Checking / Savings

Account Number: _____

Contact Info: _____

Password/PIN:_____


Name of Bank: _____

Type of Account: Checking / Savings

Account Number: _____

Contact Info: _____

Password/PIN:_____

Name of Bank: _____

Type of Account: Checking / Savings

Account Number: _____

Contact Info: _____

Password/PIN:_____


Name of Bank: _____

Type of Account: Checking / Savings

Account Number: _____

Contact Info: _____

Password/PIN:_____


Name of Bank: _____

Type of Account: Checking / Savings

Account Number: _____

Contact Info: _____

Password/PIN:_____

# **Investment Accounts:**

### Mutual Funds:

Name of Fund Manager: _____

Contact Info: _____
Account Number: _____

Password/PIN: _____


Name of Fund Manager: _____

Contact Info: _____
Account Number: _____

Password/PIN: _____


Name of Fund Manager: _____

Contact Info: _____
Account Number: _____

Password/PIN: _____

Name of Fund Manager: _____

Contact Info: _____
Account Number: _____

Password/PIN:_____


Name of Fund Manager: _____

Contact Info: _____
Account Number: _____

Password/PIN:_____


Name of Fund Manager: _____

Contact Info: _____
Account Number: _____

Password/PIN:_____

# Stocks and/or Bonds:

Name of Broker: _____

Contact Info: _____
Account Number: _____

Location of Stock Certificates: _____

Password/PIN: _____


Name of Broker: _____

Contact Info: _____
Account Number: _____

Location of Stock Certificates: _____

Password/PIN: _____

Name of Broker: _____

Contact Info: _____
Account Number: _____

Location of Stock Certificates: _____

Password/PIN: _____


Name of Broker: _____

Contact Info: _____
Account Number: _____

Location of Stock Certificates: _____

Password/PIN: _____


Name of Broker: _____

Contact Info: _____
Account Number: _____

Location of Stock Certificates: _____

Password/PIN: _____

# Pension Plans and Retirement Benefits:

<u>401K or 403b / Individual Retirement Account (IRA):</u>

Company Holding the Investment:

_____

Contact Info: _____

Account Number: _____
Password/PIN:_____

Company Holding the Investment:

_____

Contact Info: _____

Account Number: _____
Password/PIN:_____

Company Holding the Investment:

_____

Contact Info: _____

Account Number: _____
Password/PIN:_____


Company Holding the Investment:

_____

Contact Info: _____

Account Number: _____
Password/PIN:_____


Company Holding the Investment:

_____

Contact Info: _____

Account Number: _____
Password/PIN:_____

# Real Property:

Property Titled to: _____

Property Address:

_____

County and State:

_____

Mortgage held by: _____

Loan Number: _____


Property Titled to: _____

Property Address:

_____

County and State:

_____

Mortgage held by: _____

Loan Number: _____

Property Titled to: _____

Property Address:

_____

County and State:

_____

Mortgage held by: _____

Loan Number: _____


Property Titled to: _____

Property Address:

_____

County and State:

_____

Mortgage held by: _____

Loan Number: _____

# Vehicles/Boats/Aircraft:

Year/Make: _____

Model: _____

Titled to: _____

Location of Title: _____

Year/Make: _____

Model: _____

Titled to: _____

Location of Title: _____

Year/Make: _____

Model: _____

Titled to: _____

Location of Title: _____

Year/Make: _____

Model: _____

Titled to: _____

Location of Title: _____


Year/Make: _____

Model: _____

Titled to: _____

Location of Title: _____


Year/Make: _____

Model: _____

Titled to: _____

Location of Title: _____

# Social Security Benefits:

Name on Account:_____

Account Number: _____

Contact Info: _____


Name on Account:_____

Account Number: _____

Contact Info: _____


Name on Account:_____

Account Number: _____

Contact Info: _____

# Veteran's Administration (VA) Benefits:

Name on Account:_____

Account Number: _____

Contact Info: _____


Name on Account:_____

Account Number: _____

Contact Info: _____


Name on Account:_____

Account Number: _____

Contact Info: _____

# Safe Deposit Box(s):

Location of Safe Deposit Box: _____

Number of Safe Deposit Box: _____

Name of Key Holder(s): _____


Location of Safe Deposit Box: _____

Number of Safe Deposit Box: _____

Name of Key Holder(s): _____


Location of Safe Deposit Box: _____

Number of Safe Deposit Box: _____

Name of Key Holder(s): _____

# In Home or Personal Safe:

Location of Safe: _____

Combination to Safe: _____

Location of Key: _____

Name of Key Holder(s): _____


Location of Safe: _____

Combination to Safe: _____

Location of Key: _____

Name of Key Holder(s): _____


Location of Safe: _____

Combination to Safe: _____

Location of Key: _____

Name of Key Holder(s): _____

# Personal Loans Made:

Name of Person to Whom Loan Was Made:

_____

When Loan Was Made: _____
Amount of Loan: _____

Phone Number of Debtor:_____

Email Address of Debtor:_____


Name of Person to Whom Loan Was Made:

_____

When Loan Was Made: _____
Amount of Loan: _____

Phone Number of Debtor:_____

Email Address of Debtor:_____

Name of Person to Whom Loan Was Made:

_____

When Loan Was Made: _____
Amount of Loan: _____

Phone Number of Debtor:_____

Email Address of Debtor:_____


Name of Person to Whom Loan Was Made:

_____

When Loan Was Made: _____
Amount of Loan: _____

Phone Number of Debtor:_____

Email Address of Debtor:_____

# Passwords and Other Information:

Computer login Password:

_____

Email Password: _____

Cell Phone Password: _____


Passwords To Other Accounts:

Name of Account: _____
Password:_____


Name of Account: _____
Password:_____


Name of Account: _____
Password:_____

Social Media Username and Passwords:

Facebook: _____

Instagram: _____

Twitter: _____

Snapchat: _____

Tik Tok: _____

Other: _____

# Any Additional Information Or Personal Message You Would Like To Convey:

_____

_____

_____

_____

_____

_____

_____

_____

_____

_____

_____

_____

_____

_____

_____

_____

_____

_____

_____

_____

_____

_____

_____

_____

_____

_____

## Lutzel Broadway has offices in:

Charlotte, North Carolina,
Indian Trail, North Carolina,
Mooresville, North Carolina,
Myrtle Beach, South Carolina, and
Pawleys Island, South Carolina

Please call us at 704-540-0103,
Please email us at RLutzel@LutzelGandy.com

or

Visit our website at: www.LutzelBroadway.com